ONCE UPON A DREAM

South London Poets

Edited By Emily Wilson

First published in Great Britain in 2017 by:

 Young**Writers** Est. 1991

Coltsfoot Drive
Peterborough
PE2 9BF
Telephone: 01733 890066
Website: www.youngwriters.co.uk

All Rights Reserved
Book Design by Spencer Hart
© Copyright Contributors 2016
SB ISBN 978-1-78624-819-0
Printed and bound in the UK by BookPrintingUK
Website: www.bookprintinguk.com
YB0300T

FOREWORD

Welcome to 'Once Upon a Dream – South London Poets'.

For Young Writers' Key Stage Two autumn competition we invited pupils to write a poem inspired by their dreams. Poets could write about anything from their real-life aspirations and goals to a magical dream world they visit each night, maybe even a nightmare they have been trapped in. We just wanted to see how creative you could be and to encourage you to express yourselves!

Of course they meant we received a great variety of poems about all sorts of different things which were great to read. Our poets were very imaginative with the content as well as the form and you are bound to find something to suit everyone in this collection.

As always we were very pleased with the response we received from this competition and it's great to see how many pupils get involved. I would like to say a huge thank you to everyone who sent in a poem and well done to all the poets published in this collection. A special congratulations goes to *Millie Walsh* for your fantastic poem which has been selected as the winner of this book. I hope everyone published feels inspired to carry on writing and I hope to see more of your work in future competitions.

Emily Wilson

CONTENTS

Ilaria De Neiva Konig (10)	72
Eva Lynch (8)	73
Christina Galani (10)	74
Sophie Cecil (10)	75
Giulia Westermann (7)	76
Max Viventi (10)	77
Flavia Galli-Zugaro (8)	78
Adriana Moretti (9)	79
Julia Butter (9)	80
Alonga Case (9)	81
Jose Carlos Alvarez (9)	82
Adnan Al-Sadi (8)	83
Henry Butter (7)	84
Thomas Bradkin (7)	85
Joy De Selancy (8)	86
Starla Delucy Mckeeve (7)	87
Valentine Matussiere (10)	88
Carlotta Sofer (10)	89
Sofia Vialli (9)	90
Olympia Thieme Del Rio (10)	91
Orlando White (8)	92
Emma Grant-Diaz (11)	93
Sebastian Waring (7)	94
Lola Kandrac (9)	95
Mickey Maurus (7)	96
Paula Muth (8)	97
Olivia Simich (8)	98
B B Yanicelli (10)	99
Helena Titherington (10)	100
Maia Hewson (10)	101
Savanna Snell-Dyson (8)	102
Farah Parviz (8)	103
Sophia ElBishlawi (10)	104
Igor Sagiryan (10)	105
Purdy Lenigas (7)	106
Ramzi Kallini (11)	107
Taylor Demong (7)	108
Kiyaan Nathoo (8)	109
Alexander Sagiryan (8)	110
Caspian Primrose (11)	111
Celia Child-Villiers (9)	112
Gurbani Garcha (8)	113
Hugh Walsh (10)	114

Sacha Abecassis (7)	115
Allegra Collins (7)	116
Athina Vardinoyannis (8)	117
Alban Nottin (7)	118

Hill House International Junior School, London

Mika Hood (9)	119
Maya Smith (9)	120
Arabella Scanlon (10)	122
Ayla Siddiq (9)	124
Annalise Worraker (9)	126
Cate Conklin (9)	127
Chloe Stranger (9)	128
Ines Baud (9)	129
Meira Gerasimovaite (9)	130

Lucas Vale Primary School, London

Vaatsalya Swarup (9)	131
Amiri Simpson (9)	132
Jordan Charles (10)	134
Jahmari McCalla (10)	136
Mary Maina (10)	138
Aaralyn Abangma (8)	140
Jasmine Musundi-Locke (9)	141

Merton Abbey Primary School, London

Napoleon Class (10)	142
Alexandra Vicovan Ioana (10)	145
Evana Otabil (9)	146
Raulis Barsegianas (10)	148
India Francis (9)	149
Dele Oyeyele (10)	150
Jayden Brewster (9)	151
Levi Jordan Alfie Samuels (9)	152
Adam Victory (10)	154
Kize Williams (9)	155
Tharun Yogendram (9)	156
Mersedesa Barsegianaite (9)	157

Sara Salah (9)	158
Jaydhidh Yogeswaran (9)	159
Carmel Francis (9)	160
Aliyan Ahmad (9)	161
Hira Isik (10)	162
Cadey Moore (9)	163
George Brown (9)	164
Peter Sam Newell (9)	165
Khalid Dore (10)	166
Mena Kamran (9)	167
Kiril Bozhilov (9)	168
Malek Barnett (10)	169
Joanne Obeh (9)	170
Heavenly Critcher (9)	171
Erdet Dedushi (9)	172
Gabriel Hreniuc (8)	173
Sadie Marsham (9)	174
Goncalo Monteiro (8)	175
Patryk Slusarczyk (9)	176
Layla Al-Bayati (8)	177
Pola Czekaj (9)	178
Cherry Bernard (9)	179
Aran Amin (9)	180
David Tyczynski (9)	181
Kacey Fisher (9)	182
Charlie Fraser (9)	183

St John's Walworth CE Primary School, London

Ana Maria Dumitru	184
Jamila Ricketts (7)	185

THE POEMS

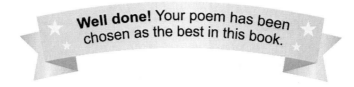

Well done! Your poem has been chosen as the best in this book.

Nightmares

Wolf is howling, witch is cackling,
Children over orange fires, roasting, crackling.
Zombies rising, skeletons creaking,
Hiding under thin covers, timidly peeking.
Noises in the dead of night,
Things that make you jump in fright.
Darkest black like a raven's wing,
Swallowing up everything.
Vampires in castles, my blood they sup,
Argh!
It's a good thing I woke up!

Millie Walsh (10)
Garden House School, London

Undertopia

I have travelled far and wide,
As well as hardly at all.
But this is my most special story,
Which can even be read to the ones who are small.
I started at the beach,
With the sand covering my toes.
And my dear old dog, Marcel,
Sniffing with his nose!
My aunt was taking pictures,
Of the endless sea,
While the strange dog named Wildness,
Was standing next to me.
I curiously leapt through the air,
To find myself in water.
I noticed my flicking tail,
And heard the sound of laughter.
The others were all floating there,
My Aunt Sinead just sighed.
The dogs howled in despair,
They did not seem to notice,
Their marvellous, beautiful fins.
So, I just swam quite deeper,
I nearly got caught by a creeper.
And there, right there,

I held my breath,
And found the strangest sight.
There was a spellbinding kingdom,
Much to my delight.
A mermaid girl swam up to me,
And this is what she said, with lots of glee!
'Oh, come with me and you will see!
But first let's get your friend, oh please!'
We swam straight back,
They quickly followed,
She said again, 'Come on! I'll bring you to my hollow!'
Soon afterwards, we ate some lunch,
I had seaweed and scallops,
For a quick munch!
And that was when
The disaster came,
Slowly rumbling up from the halls of fame.
We all gasped,
But Sinead stood strong,
Oh gosh. Oh my,
I thought I would cry!
This monstrous devil,
This terrible creature,
His massive tail,
It swept along,
Smashing tables.

Very wrong!
The thing picked up Melinda, our mermaid friend,
And shook her around like a rattle's end.
Sinead, the hero, furiously swam up,
She punched the bully thoroughly,
And took a dagger-sharp rock.
Her aim was absolute perfection,
Her speed was right on time.
It hit the monster's heart!
The thing fell to the ground,
'The monster is now dead!'
I heard the villagers shout,
As they lifted her in the air,
No one giving doubt.
They held a great festival,
And the king grandly vowed,
'This day is to become a tradition!'
Shouted Sinead,
Out loud!

Sibeal De Barra Penman (10)
Garden House School, London

4

The Mystery Of The World

Sitting in the rocket I heard the countdown, 5, 4, 3, 2, 1, blast-off!
I shot into the world of mystery, the glinting moon shone as its reflection did the same.
The stars whizzed past the fiery rocket.
The galaxy is big but my wonder is bigger.
The emptiness of the world and the darkness of it got hold of me
And made me realise what a dazzling world I live in,
And what a wonderful family that encourages me to do amazing things.
The brightness of the stars dazzled into my eyes
As the sun shone like it was a golden angel.
The sparkle in my eye glinted as tears of joy danced down my pink cheeks as my lips trembled.
I thought my dream will come true and I will see the moon, the stars and the golden angel.
As she flutters, she will keep on waiting until she finds another little girl or boy who has a good dream and who will make it come true.

Iris Mowbray (9)
Garden House School, London

My Dream Begins

It was as hot and humid as a fire.
I dashed over the hill
and just a few miles away,
was a bushy forest.
I sprinted and sprinted,
fell to the ground under a giggling willow tree
which was dancing a Hula from Hawaii.
The spaghetti lines of the willow tree tickled
my burnt shoulder.
I darted my eyes at the sky,
massaging my pulled thigh
and there were clouds swimming through the sun.
I hobbled into the forest,
on the left side fairies were playing mini tennis
and on the right side, witches cast spells on pixies.
In the middle of the witches
and fairies appeared an ancient, wooden door.
I opened it slowly with dread,
I got a shock - *Charlie, my teddy bear?* I asked myself.
He asked me if I could join him on his journey to
Candyland kingdom.
I said yes.
After a few hours, we arrived at the candy castle
which was made from sticky toffee pudding.

It was so cute, I just wanted to eat it up.
We walked down a liquorice carpet
towards the throne, made of popcorn and brownies.
The king was made of brownie for the upper body,
chocolate sticks for legs and a jawbreaker for head
and he gave Charlie a chocolate medal.

Alexandra Ter Haar (9)
Garden House School, London

The Dark Castle

I dreamt of a dark castle,
On a vast, green field.
Luscious land as far as I can see,
Though a dark castle lies ahead of me.
One not pleasing,
One not nice,
But one that would tickle my vice.
What could I do?
Whatever could there be?
Wizards and witches,
Fiends and foes,
Knights and dragons,
Maybe even the round table!
I frantically set off,
My heart filled with excitement,
And then a fortunate enlightenment.
When I arrived at the shadow of the fortress,
To my great surprise,
The door, which reveals the mighty inside, welcomed
me with glowing eyes.
A collection of swords lie in front of me,
Shimmering, glistening in my face.
Suddenly, my vision fixed on a platter saying, 'Thee
shall try these.'

Through the alleyways and flights of stairs gloomy,
The rooms were vast and roomy for pretend sword-
fighting and dare-devilling.
Unexpectedly, with a clash of swords, Sir Lancelot's
dusty armour fell upon me and crumbled! *Crash!*
I awoke!

Azlan Khan (9)
Garden House School, London

My Ponies And Me

Riders were on their horses
Yet I was the only one
Racing through the obstacle courses
It was so much more than just fun.

The dog starts to bark
The crowd goes crazy and claps
The brown-feathered lark
Sings whilst he flaps

Sage neighs with pride
I scanned my surroundings closely
I immediately let out a huge, long sigh
As people scurried to approach me.

After everyone left
I leaned against the candyfloss tree
To realise I was the best
I slumped and hugged my knee.

The twinkling sun
Smiled at me
All this was now done
It was just my ponies and me.

Now the meadows were all in peace
It was just my ponies and me
Now the content has settled down
It was just my ponies and me

Now the farm has shut down
It was just my ponies and me
My ponies and me.

Uma Kumar (10)
Garden House School, London

Alien Hunt In Space

S o lonely in space... *Crash!* Is that a flying saucer? There must be an alien, there it is!

P *itter patter pit pat,* you know I'm going to stay here instead of run after an emerald alien, anyway the moon is made of candyfloss.

A ah, there it is again, I'm going to follow it... where is that cheeky alien?

C ream, yummy, I need to eat some, I've been chasing this alien for an hour.

E nough, where is this alien?

H a, there is the alien. 'Hello, I'm Luna Starlight.' 'I'm Matilde Busse.'

'U nbelievable,' I exclaimed, 'can we be friends?' 'Sure Luna.'

N ow me and Luna are friends, we moved to her planet called Allamsim.

'T wilight is my baby sister and Starla is my big sister,' introduced Luna.

Matilde Al Shauof (8)
Garden House School, London

Climbing In The Clouds

My amazing dreams usually begin as they always do,
With the ripe, overgrown scent of coconuts falling from
the luminous, tall palm trees swishing and swaying in
the fruity wind.
The waves sprinkling and drizzling down on the
giggling golden flakes.
A large rainbow coming out of the overgrown jungle.
Glittery, golden sand the colour of the fiery orb.
All the coconuts were sunbathing under the palm trees.
When you climbed up the stunning rainbow, your heart
fluttered like a colourful butterfly.
You could smell tiny, little flowers as rare as gold.
The sound coming from the heavens sounded like a
sweet lullaby.
The clouds were as fluffy as a soft rabbit and they were
dancing with pride.
I saw Pegasus galloping in front of my small eye.
It was so beautiful, a tear drizzles down my eye.
The same thing happens every single night.

Laila Bennett (9)
Garden House School, London

My Horse

'Gary, Gary,' I said to my horse,
'Let's go and win Badminton Horse Trials, of course!'
'Let's start practising now,' I said,
As Gary stood shaking his head.
'Oh, come on,' I screeched in a high-pitched voice,
'It is not that bad and you have no choice!'

We set off to the yard to get tacked up.
'The girth does not fit, that's such bad luck!'
I popped to the shop to take a look
And I saw one hanging on a hook.
I zoomed inside and took it off.
As I paid for it, I got 20% off.

We got there at last, it was such a blast.
Badminton Horse Trials.
As I was waiting to compete,
I could feel my body shivering above my feet.
As the speaker said my name,
It was time to up my game...

Iris Kimmins (9)
Garden House School, London

The Candy Experience Land!

Once upon a dream, there was a delicious candyland
with cookie houses, smooth, creamy and fluffy icing as
the rooftop and marshmallow windows.
There was also a chocolate bar as the chimney.
The sky was as pink as blossoms.
The river was going *swish! swish! swish!*
There was a scrumptious, delicious, curly and tasty
candyfloss talking and jumping in the air.
The butterfly flew through the sky and made a sound
that sounded like *flap, flap, flap!*
The wood on the trees looked like hard caramel.
Instead of clouds in the sky, there were ruby-red hearts
flying through the sky.
Instead of grass on the floor, there were chocolate
Smarties covered all over the floor.
All the mountains were made of ice cream and
chocolate sauce on top.
All dreams come true in Candyland!

Eva Dramitinos (7)
Garden House School, London

The Battlefield Nightmare

I can hear the shouts and cries of the wounded and I feel pity as they die.
As I see the gods fighting and massive amounts of creatures retreat into the woods, anger fills my heart.
The soil is red with blood from the dead.
The midnight moon stares in horror as, one by one, life retreats from the bodies of the dead.
From my Pegasus, I see many forms of death, illness, bloody death and many, many more.
There is blood as red as wine and giants as big as mountains toppling over.
The gods' beloved would be heartbroken with sorrow as their husbands were killed.
I feel horrified as spears, swords, axes and arrows glance off creatures' bodies.
I feel almost relieved as I fall to the ground, slipping off my Pegasus for this seemed like the end of life.
For everything.

Sam Wildman (7)
Garden House School, London

Candy Land

Lemonade is what we swim in.
Splash, there goes me.
I have to say, this lemonade is good.
There's me and my friends bobbing on marshmallows
in the lemonade.
There we are, getting really sticky with the candyfloss
stuck to us.
Hey guys look, there is the tallest slide in the world.
It is as if it is never-ending.
Just for your safety, beware of the
green bubblegum monsters.
Guess what? All the sweets are healthy.
The sweets there are exquisite and magnificent.
The best thing is that there are edible unicorns,
But they grow back to life when you eat them!
The sun is as bright as a hot, yellow furnace.
So, when I want to go to my dream,
I have a special key that will guide me.

Trinity Delucy Mclawe (10)
Garden House School, London

A Magical Land

In a land far, far away,
There were three humongous islands,
It all started when...

The world went *bang!*
And made these islands,
Joining with bridges.

I first stepped by
And I saw a girl, Katarina,
She walked up to me,
We got talking, Katarina and I.

We also found Kayla,
We got talking,
Kayla and I.

'Beware!' said a sign,
We ignored it and went in,
We saw a shape moving in the air,
What is it? 'Don't know!'

Deeper and deeper,
'Argh!' screamed Kayla,
'It's g-g-g-ghosts, run!'

We're back home,
Safely in my dream,
I hear, 'Beware, beware, beware!'

Isabella Cruickshank (8)
Garden House School, London

Dream World Of A Dolphin

My dream world is a magical world.
Step into my exciting world as a mom giving birth to a
newborn baby.
My world is as beautiful as a sparkling rainbow which
smiled like a tiny fairy.
In the sky, there are fireflies.
I can see a candyfloss king.
My world has a touch of emerald green to it.
My dream world has a giant marshmallow king who
always makes me smile.
My dream world can dance as good as a professional
tap dancer.
My best friend is as amazed as a newborn baby
discovering the Earth's secrets.
My brother is as astonished as a child getting a real
fairy in a Kinder Surprise.
My mom is as kind as a gentle, wise lady.
In my world, my friend is as delighted as a girl finding
her inspiring new inspiration.

Isha Khemka (7)
Garden House School, London

Take A Look In The Dream Jar

If I could fly with the larks,
We could tour London's parks,
If I could dance with a flamingo,
We could go to a pink disco,
If I could jump with a kangaroo,
I'd jump much higher than you,
If I could run with the cheetahs,
In my race, I'd be the fastest over 100 metres,
If I could swim with a fish,
This would be, by far, my greatest wish,
If I could camouflage with a chameleon,
Orange is the best colour that suits us, in my opinion,
If I could climb with a monkey,
This would be awesome, amazing and quirky,
If I could flutter with the butterflies,
Amongst the bright blue sky,
Now it's time to close the dream jar,
In this poem we've travelled near and far.

Alexia Flick (10)
Garden House School, London

Above The Clouds

Take a trip into the sky, see a unicorn, see it fly.
In the heaven of luscious sky,
You never think of saying goodbye.
Meet its family, see its house,
And please don't forget your colourful blouse.
One of the unicorns is called Zouse,
Another wants me to see its house.
One has a very new spouse,
That has golden hair and a super big mouth.
Nous the unicorn wants to take me to the south.
And along the way we picked up a cake,
It was an immensely good bake.
It had little wings, the colour of a lake so it could fly...
Now say hello and say goodbye,
Jump down the rainbow out of the sky.
This is not the end, this is just beginning,
Don't say bye, just say hi!

Mary MacGreevy (10)
Garden House School, London

Dreams

Dreams are here and there.
In our sleep they're not rare but they do have crazy subjects like a talking mare.
Roaming everywhere are dreams,
In my dreams I am in the Olympics with a gold medal and matching gold hair.
Even in this fairy-tale land where rainbows are chocolate and mermaids are real,
Where you never forgot the friendly smiles and the silver goblet
And in the orange juice lake and star trees below,
The valleys are Cadbury and the sea is milkshake.
My dog and cat are curled up in a magical land.
Their names are Lollie and Candyman.
As Lollie lay down, he gave a small growl,
Which made Candy leap up and that was a foul.
She fell in a pond and needed a towel.

Madeline Tyrer (9)
Garden House School, London

Deadly Animal

The deadly animal called John lived in a dreamland,
That everything was strange, like a rat would eat cats,
And a worm would eat birds and boys wear skirts,
That was the dreamland, that was the dreamland.

John was spitting fire, John was getting higher,
My open mouth became drier and I much shyer,
I was scared, scared and terrified,
I shouldn't have escaped my house in
the darkest night.

Braveness must rule or a bit of Kung Fu,
I punch my fist against this awful John,
And for not too long he was dead,
So I could go back to my bed.

Turning around, trying to find back my sleep,
Hoping my next dream will be more sweet.

Max Muth (9)
Garden House School, London

Sweet Dreams

As I shut my eyes every night,
I drift off to a magical sight.

When I arrive,
I feel so alive.

As joy fills me,
I feel so free.

As volcanoes erupt with butter cream,
I feel as if I'm going to scream.

As I catch the sight of a chocolate stream,
The sun shines with a great beam.

As I see a chocolate flake,
I do not want to awake.

As I see a marshmallow toad,
I feel as if I'm going to explode.

As sherbet raindrops fall,
I feel as if I'm growing tall.

I don't want to leave this in my head,
And wake up in my own little bed.

Isabella Rassmuson (11)
Garden House School, London

Sweets

My house is made from gingerbread,
It has red and white candy canes on the front of
the house,
A pink jelly door and also a cream roof with
lots of icing.
There was a chocolate river like a chocolate cookie,
The mountains were as beautiful as an emerald.
I even got to pop a lollipop in my mouth.
I also accidentally knocked down a chocolate tree over
into the queen of sweets.
It was very weird in the land of sweets because sweety
people could read, sing, dance, run and play.
The slices were as beautiful as pink diamonds dancing
on the ball.
The skies were filled with rainbows.
The playgrounds were as joyful as the first ever
laughter that ever was.

Angeline Daniel-Graff (7)
Garden House School, London

Heaven Rainbow

The three kittens jumping over the beautiful and bright
rainbow in Heaven.
The first cat was Pipoca, the second was Lulu,
the third was Sunny.
'We don't need money for grace,' said God
When I looked up, I saw the chest dancing and floating
like a butterfly
And then, *bong*, the kittens went on the rainbow
up in Heaven.
They were so fluffy and muffy I couldn't bear it.
Then Pipoca started miaowing.
I looked up and she was all in jewels
And, to my surprise, they all were graced by God.
Then a cod in the pond popped up like popcorn
jumping in the pan.
Grace for the three kittens jumping over the rainbow
in Heaven.

Mia Pastore (8)
Garden House School, London

My Dream Began As They All Do

I could see little birds made out of cupcakes.
Singing words and eating nutcakes and homes made out of sweets.
They looked as juicy as a peach.
Whenever I walked through this lovely town,
I saw koalas saying, 'How do you do? I'm bound to meet you.'
And I saw this big tree made out of milk chocolate and glee.
I looked inside this fab thing and suddenly saw these cheeses with wings.
And then I walked out of glee tree and found this forest in front of me.
I walked into the splendid forest and met this banana named Morist.
We went together into this home made out of a cone.
We lived together forever.
With the banana and me and a random bee.

Ophelia Mayhew (9)
Garden House School, London

A Castle Under The Sea

Deep, deep down,
Under the crashing waves,
Stands a brilliant crown,
Surrounded by caves.

A magnificent glittering jewel,
Encrusted with shimmering pearls,
A place where mermen come to duel,
And diamonds are shaped in curls.

With a flick of my tail,
I'm within a regal room,
With magical whales,
All swept clean with a broom.

I twirl and I dance,
In a crystal ballroom,
I flounce and I prance,
And my long hair I groom.

Enchanted by the music,
Entranced by the light,
I flip and I kick to the beat of the night,
To the beat of the dreamy night.

Ariana Murphy (10)
Garden House School, London

Olympic Dream

Standing on the Olympic floor,
My heart pumping as fast as it had never been before.
This was my chance to show off and dance,
As I presented, everyone cheered as loud as they could
And as loud as I could hear.
I had done my flip, my split and now my other
triple front flip,
All that was left was the dismount with
the double backflip.
I finished my dismount perfect and clean,
I really wanted to win, but what about my team?
As they called the final results, first place
Carolina Rassmuson.
I was jumping up and down with joy,
I really was enjoying this.
My team also came first,
Boy, this was paradise.

Carolina Rassmuson (9)
Garden House School, London

My Dream Of Space

I dreamt a dream of outer space,
It really is a marvellous place,
We travelled at the speed of light,
That really was my favourite flight,
We landed on the planet Mars,
And gazed up at the many stars,
I thought I saw a Martian too,
It took us to the Martian zoo,
Oh dear, oh my, but what is that?
It really looks just like a cat.
Except its hair is long and brown,
Its mouth is in an ugly frown,
In fact, it looks just like my sis,
I wondered what to make of this,
And then I woke up to see her head,
Away she flew back to her bed,
I recommend you go to space,
Just go right now and pack your case.

Fiorella Beausang-Hunter (10)
Garden House School, London

Can You Imagine...

Once again I was dreaming,
It started as usual,
I was taking a stroll in the garden,
When I thought, *I beg your pardon,*
As I stared at the hole in the ground down below,
And jumped in and sunk in, *boom!*
I landed on the ground,
I was in a world that hadn't been found,
I strutted along with the birds for a song...
I heard a noise,
I stood up with poise as I reached higher and higher,
My footsteps got slower and slower,
So I got down on my knees,
'Oh stay with me, I beg you please!'
I was free, I got delivered as He bent over me.

Grace Stolkin (10)
Garden House School, London

The Land Of My Dreams

Step into the land of mine.
The first sight you would see is the sight of candy.
Trees have turned into cotton candy
But the best thing of all is that the trees can burp.
And when it rains mints, the thunder comes out and it
roars like a lion roaring for help.
If you want to see the extraordinary house of mine,
then follow me.
It has beautiful walls made of thick and
scrumptious cookies.
And if you want a bite out of it then you have to
get permission.
The chimney is a rainbow-coloured straw and no
ordinary smoke comes out.
It's what you want to come out of it.
Dairy Milk smoke is coming out now.

Reilly Murphy (7)
Garden House School, London

Dream

I fell asleep and woke up in my dream.
This is my favourite dream!
It's the dream where there are wish trees.
Everywhere pink grass that does a dance.
And a pink mansion and other things in
my lovely dream!
Melting chocolate rivers that glimmer.
Shops with tops everywhere that make everyone stare
At the bags and shoes that make everyone say oooh!
The best thing about this dream is nothing's normal.
My dog's a cat that miaows.
I have a mansion and better fashion credit cards
And my BFF is a banana!
But now I'm missing my normal cat and family
so pinch me!

Honor Taylor (9)
Garden House School, London

Bubble Trouble

Suddenly, the spotlight blinded me, my forehead was glinting from the light reflecting off my sweat.
After a while, I got calmer and started baking.
I added a pinch of mewweed, unicorn snot, pickled imprings, pixie poo and obviously too many good dreams.
The mixture began to bubble, then it started to fizz, then pop, then it cracked and eventually, it blew!
A disgusting rotten egg, mouldy cheese, pongy smell was produced, then a baby unicorn appeared and it was beautiful.
It let me clip its toenails (which was the last ingredient).
Then I popped in the toenails, mixed and stirred the bake and won the contest.

Pia Kebell (9)
Garden House School, London

The Cloud Star

T iny shooting stars surround me,

H owling, my dog, for we are stuck in the middle of space on a cloud,

E ast, north, south, west, nothing but stars and clouds,

C orner to corner but in the last corner there lies a cloud in

L ove in the shape of a star,

O ver the moon we go to the cloud,

U nderstanding for crying,

D one!' he says, for his favourite friend, the star,

S tar, oh the star,

'T is true, the star is dead,

A heavy tear drops down,

R ain of a cloud.

Savannah Sibony (8)
Garden House School, London

Soaring Through Space On A Pegasus

Soaring through space on Pegasus,
Feels much better than a bus,
The Milky Way stretched afar,
Quite unlike the chocolate bar,
The centre of the Milky Way,
The glowing core, it looked my way,
That big, bright ball of glowing gas,
I could not imagine its incredible mass,
The rings of Saturn in all their glory,
Seemed to tell me an ancient story,
But the planet itself, another thing,
Even more impressive than its rocky ring,
It called to me,
I giggled with glee,
With a clatter of hooves,
Much harder than shoes,
We landed on the lonely ball.

Miranda McLaughlan (10)
Garden House School, London

The Monster

There was once a prince as handsome as can be,
Naming the land and naming the sea.
He did not care for others,
Not his mother,
Not his sister, not his father
And not his brothers.
So, one day a woman as old as can be,
Travelled through his land and travelled through
his sea.
Until she banged on his door with a rock, rock, rock,
And he opened the door and said,
'What? What? What?'
She pleaded and pleaded to have something
hot to eat,
And he said, 'No! No! No!'
So she turned him into a beast,
And he ate her for his feast.

Lucinda Delucy Mckeeve (8)
Garden House School, London

Floating Island

My dream began the same as any other,
My imagination,
I was on a floating island covered in luscious greenery,
Little flowers danced in the wind,
Smiling as I passed,
The smell of ripe fruit filled my nose,
As I dashed towards the trees
The birds came and the birds went,
Birds sang and birds flew,
Birds tweet their greeting to you,
The grey smudges floated up and up,
As if asking me to come and follow them,
I leaped into the sky,
Hoping, hoping that I might just fly,
And you know what?
I did
I flew right up to the moon and back.

Alexia Wilson (9)
Garden House School, London

Hogwarts

The Hogwarts express took me on board,
Everything except my mum and dad snored,
I wasn't very scared at all,
Because I had all my friends aboard,
Harry, Ron and Hermione were their names,
Harry had Hedwig, Ron had Scabbers and I had Lame,
Lame was an owl that was very smart,
But he ate a lot of blueberry tart,
And when he raced, he'd always win,
But sometimes he got stuck in a very large tin,
When we got off, we saw a massive castle over a lane,
But when we came in, it looked bigger for its name,
It was scary with big moving stairs.

Carl Girard (7)
Garden House School, London

Unicorns On Mars

Unicorns on Mars are as soft as a puppy
Now another unicorn has landed on Mars
In space, nobody knows if there are unicorns on Mars
Come to Mars! See for yourself, I now know
Oh, three humans in a rocket
Run for your lives
Now the unicorns have gone to the moon
Soon they will be called unicorns on the moon.

Oh no, I hate it, I want to be on Mars
Now I will never be known ever again
My friends will call me names
Oh no, I don't want to be called names
Rockets are mean, I do not like it
So now the name is Unicorns on the Moon.

Daisy Malmberg (8)
Garden House School, London

A Year In A Dream

I have drifted to sleep
And in my dream I see
A forest of pale flower buds
Sleepily bursting into
Blossoms of cherry blossom.

Oh, it's changing, I see
Fresh, green leaves
Being pulled by the wind
On a bright, sunny day.

The leaves are turning
Gold and red,
The gold leaves start to dance
On the breeze.

When all the leaves are gone
It is winter and snow has woken
And snowflakes gracefully start falling down.
It is the end of the year
And about to start again.

Susanna Westin (8)
Garden House School, London

The Minotaur And Pegasus

The Minotaur and Pegasus played football on the sun,
They both tried hard but Pegasus won!

I watched as the referee fired his gun,
Pegasus was quick - what was to be done?

The Minotaur tried every trick he knew,
In spite of it all, he only scored a few!

He puffed and he panted until he was blue,
He couldn't keep up, that was true!

Pegasus sped to victory,
The Minotaur lost so angrily.

What a day, what a sight to see,
I loved the match and I watched with glee!

Guglielmo Belingheri (9)
Garden House School, London

My Dream Comes True

I look at the audience around me,
And feel a spark of glee,
The whistle goes and it's time to flee,
I dive in, feeling free.

The water around me is blue and crystal clear,
I'm sprinting with energy in a fast, fast gear,
I seem to have lost all sense of fear,
I touch the wall and I hear an enormous cheer.

The audience breaks into a song,
The swim felt like it went on for so long,
I then hear the final *ding dong*,
I shed a tear of happiness as the medal gets
carried along.

Melinda Aznar (10)
Garden House School, London

My Monster

It's there,
I can feel its longing stare,
Piercing my body like a knife,
Waiting,
For its time to strike,
I dare not breathe,
I can't even shout and, even when I try,
no words come out,
The fear inside me swells and grows and a tingle runs
from my spine to my toes,
Its presence is silent, its eyes alight, burning like fire
throughout the night,
My heart pounds like a clicking loom but then I stop,
'Hey! This is my room!'
I swivel my head,
And leap from my bed,
It's gone.

Olympia White (10)
Garden House School, London

Riding A Unicorn

The sun was smiling at us,
Gazing out across the land, unicorns galloping
towards us.
Marshmallow mountains frowning at the sun,
I felt the sun pinching me,
While setting a lion free.
Gathering up my braveness, I stepped up on a unicorn,
The unicorn bolted off like lightning,
It was very frightening.
Suddenly, it launched into the air,
Leaving Ivy sitting there.
Soon, we were flying across the sky,
Gliding in the wind,
Like a leaf falling from a tree, we swiftly glided
back down.

Sally Niedringhaus (9)
Garden House School, London

The Haunted House

As I glided across the white blanket, a shiver shivered up my spine.
I was standing in a spooky house and a mouse scattered around the dark, wooden floor.
Shadows surrounded me.
The trees were whispering in my ear.
I was in fear from head to toe.
Low voices whistled around the haunted house.
Leaves crackled!
Spiders crawled...
I wrapped my coat tighter and tighter,
I felt way more heated.
Suddenly, a pain ached through my neck as it led down to my heart.
I screamed and that was the end.

Alexia Abecassis (9)
Garden House School, London

Untitled

In the land where I live,
I have all I want where it's fun,
I love all that I want and have,
Including doughnuts and marshmallows and a bun,
All that I want.

I do not want to be annoyed,
I do not want to be bit,
I do not want to be out of nice rooms,
I do not want to be hit,
All that I want.

Well, I have not to speak,
I automatically just get what I want,
I love my comfortable chair,
It has not a single slant,
Well, also that is what I like.

Charles Nasser (7)
Garden House School, London

Here We Go

It was midnight
when the clock struck,
the clouds were dark
there was a black mark,
at sunrise the sky turned pink
all of the clouds would link,
the Pegasus flew
with wings such colours, who would know, who?
I stood on the clouds with pride
and made sure my hair was tied,
Peg the Pegasus came
with a golden mane,
a smile crawled across my face
I climbed on, checking my lace,
we flew until the sun was up
when I came home, I slept like a lump,
goodnight clouds.

Maya Woolf (10)
Garden House School, London

Marshmallows Are Silly

Far, far away in an alien's mouth lived a planet.
In that planet was a marshmallow who lived in a
very cool house.
It was on a cloud, it was made out of rainbows.
It had a sticky toffee door like honey.
Its roof was made of squishy candyfloss.
The marshmallow climbed up the edible vines.
Then jumped into a huge coconut and went to space.
At space, the marshmallow bit the moon in half and
ate it for tea.
Smash! The marshmallow fell off the moon and landed
on a roller coaster.

Eugenia Davenbart (9)
Garden House School, London

Nightmare In Wonderland

Being transported to a strange new land,
It was just not what I'd planned!
I opened my eyes in a gleaming meadow,
A gigantic castle towering like the shadow
Of an angry, giant ready for a fight.
The castle stood, lighting up the night,
Shooting fireballs that gave me a fright.
So I sprinted away with all my might.
When I looked up to see,
I noticed a bright angel cradling me.
The next day, I woke up in my bed,
Fireballs, angels and castles still swirling
around my head.

Poppy Duncan (10)
Garden House School, London

Alone In The Ocean

I am lost,
So alone and afraid,
My ship has sunk,
There is nothing left but me and my soul,
Fear grasping my senses,
I can't even think straight,
Hallucinations crawling into my eyes,
Oh, I wish I wouldn't die,
Great white sharks coming into my vision,
Help! I need to make the right decision,
Sharks are multiplying,
I don't know what to do,
Closer the sharks are coming,
I wish I could start running,
One of them has bitten me,
Now it is all over.

Isis Dob (10)
Garden House School, London

The Fairground

Riding on the Ferris wheel
Coming down I heard a squeal
It wasn't her or him or them
It was just me
Well, Anna's on the spooky ride
So I'll just take a stride
To go onto the Mouse Hunter
Screaming as my carriage rode along
I waved my hands into the air and sang
my favourite song
Just then the carriage stopped
What happened?
Was I stuck?
I started getting panicked
When then I started turning and tossing
Then, *snap!*
It was the end.

Sofya Sukhoruchkina (10)
Garden House School, London

The Haunted House

When I go to sleep on a stormy night,
I wake up in my dream alright.
The darkness flashes with the children around,
There's a girl called Bella and her brother, Jake
They are around me as I wait.
As we enter the haunted house, the thunder goes
flash, *kaboom!*
We are not safe in here, a knife on the ground,
A whirly thing is around me now.
Goodbye Bella and Jake,
Hope to see you again.
As I wake up in the rain,
I've been sleepwalking again!

Esme Leasor (8)
Garden House School, London

The Mountains

The dogs panted.
You could hear their pitter-patter.
I planted myself in the corner of the sled
Under warm blankets.
The snowflakes danced gleefully.
The river didn't flow; it looked like silk
About to be woven on a loom.

The sky was inky black.
You could see shooting stars attack
The sky gleaming gracefully.

The face of the mountain is bold.
It snows again.
When the rain turns to sleeping snow,
I feel dreamy. I fall asleep.

Lily Root (8)
Garden House School, London

When I Grow Up

When I grow up I'm going to be a taxi driver,
When I grow up I'm going to be richer than a king,
When I grow up I'm going to be a fancy footballer,
When I grow up I'm going to be an amazing footballer,
When I grow up I'm going to be a
fast basketball player,
When I grow up I'm going to be a singer,
When I grow up I'm going to be a video game maker,
When I grow up I'm going to be an illustrator,
When I grow up I'm going to be an author.

Adebayo Ogan-Cole (7)
Garden House School, London

Unicorn Universe

As I swam in the melted marshmallows
I saw those pretty little fellows
Of course they're unicorns, don't get me wrong
They're smooth as silk and sweet as a song
I smelt delicious, sticky caramel
As I stopped, I fell into a chocolate well
I jumped on cotton candy clouds
And bellowed my hellos loudly and clearly
To my sugary sweet friend who was on the other end
I felt free with glee
As my mind told me,
This is the place I should be.

Haya Al Zawawi (10)
Garden House School, London

The Problems In Space

There's lots of problems in space, let me tell you a few,
One is there are flying pumpkins,
Jelly as Jupiter,
A mango as Mars
And a giant avocado as the sun,
Also liquorice as the whole universe.
When you go in a rocket, it's not a normal rocket,
It's made from candyfloss to candy cane.
Also, when you hit a planet you sink right in and pop
out the other side.
The last huge problem is aliens wander
around everywhere, riding on unicorns or griffins.

Zoe Reichhelm (8)
Garden House School, London

My Dream Land

M y dream land is the best in the universe,

Y ellow, blue, maybe violet too, it can become any colour you want it to.

D electable since it is edible,

R ecurring beauty,

E verlasting life,

A mazingly vast,

M outh-wateringly scrummy,

L ovely landscapes that can look like nothing you could possibly imagine,

A erodynamic birds,

N erdy,

D ream Land is simply wonderful!

Daisy Marsden (8)
Garden House School, London

Safari

On the safari there were lots of animals
Like elephants that were grey as a thunder cloud,
Eyes as brown as chocolate and
A lion with a mane as fluffy as candyfloss.
They saw a snake as slimy as a khaki tank talking.
A springing buck who looked as beautiful as
a dancing rose,
A baby rhinoceros as jumpy as a kangaroo bouncing
across the African plains.
It was the best safari anyone had ever been on in their
whole, entire lives.

Ava Stolkin (8)
Garden House School, London

My Dream World

In my dream world there is a big castle with rich chocolate brick walls.
Rice paper windows and a cake roof.
There are lollipop trees as tall as giraffes.
There is also a humongous smiling sun and a big balloon mountain.
Did you know that there is also a wonderful starlight panda dancing and singing a lullaby at the end of the hilltops.
In the distance you can see that castle, glamorous and cool.
Would you like to see it?
Well, I'm not stopping you.

Evelyn Stride (8)
Garden House School, London

Dream Land

D ream Land, Dream Land, the best place to be, now you see.
R olling over clouds, it's like swimming in the sea, *swish, sway.*
E verything is lovely, it's the best place to be.
A t Dream Land you won't feel low.
M ostly you know, but how do we go?

L ovely Dream Land.
A nd I don't know how to go but...
N ever ever give up.
D ream Land, Dream Land, the best place to be.

Freedom Afriyie (8)
Garden House School, London

62

The Fly Dance

T he fly dance is a very fun dance.
H eld on planet Dream
E agles soar in the sky

F or a lovely dream.
L ovely dream it will make you have
Y um yum case it makes you want to

D ance and dance and dance the fly dance every day.
A lthough she's a flying horse and her friend is a
peacock
N ever they fight.
C lue number one
E veryone loves the fly dance.

Maya Navon (8)
Garden House School, London

The Snakes And The Man

Now I have a poem all about a snake,
Once or twice a day he likes a piece of steak,
For he likes to write on his list with his quill,
Who he lets live and who he lets be killed,
For the slithering one doesn't look like a nice guy,
But even if he has a hypnotising staff,
He is extremely kind,
For if you come to his base with door handles as fangs,
His home looks extremely small with his
king cobra stand,
But actually has a gigantic band!

Andreas Reichhelm (7)
Garden House School, London

My Candy Dream World

If you step into my world,
You will see small popping candy flowing down like drops and make a big crash on the ground.
The candy plays One Direction on the drums.
The pistachio-green cream is as delicious as freshly baked apple pie.
Lollipops go *plop!*
They are like flowers on a tree.
Purple popping candy grass!
It sort of makes the ground wobble a bit.
Sadly, the big, big, big corn moon went *bang* on the land and it ended!

Sophia Thomas (7)
Garden House School, London

Cloud Island

My dream began as they all do,
Floating slowly across the sky, my cloud shimmering,
The cloud's population was little, white, fluffy bunnies,
The scent of rain dashed around me,
Tickling my feet softly,
The silky-furred bunnies jumped around excitedly,
I gasped as a pink, fluffy unicorn floated by,
A golden unicorn landed next to me,
It was giving me a look to say, 'Ride me.'
I jumped on and we rode through the island.

Isabelle Long (10)
Garden House School, London

The Bolt!

Around me came a blinding light,
I sat up with a jolt just to hear an outbreak of a fight,
In the castle...
I looked around just to see,
The universe had come with me,
And I was on a comet, looked around and
saw some comets,
Above me loomed a castle,
I ran inside with a shudder,
To make the outline of a floating rudder,
There came a clatter of bones,
To see a zombie with cones,
And a dead cat in the castle.

Marco Castelvetri (8)
Garden House School, London

The Nightmare

Suddenly, I appeared
In the middle of nowhere
I was walking with my dog
And my friend called Bob.

Bob's mouth dropped open
And sprinted back home
I started to swim in the misty river
In front of me swam a school
Of horrifying piranhas.

We were in a tropical jungle
Walking away from the deserted village
Anxiously, I ran out of the water
A long snake curled around my slim leg.

Max Valkor (9)
Garden House School, London

Why Do We Dream?

Is a dream a reality or not?
Do we see what we dream or not?
When I so often plummet to the bare, bare ground,
I see nothing but darkness with my round, round eyes.
Yet still I live to see it once more,
Why? Do we dream to seek something that we do not
with our blind, blind eyes?
Do we dream to stop terrible disasters
Or do we dream to make it for ourselves?
Why do we dream?
Do we dream?
What is a dream?

Arun Lal (10)
Garden House School, London

Path On Stars

I am walking on stars
The moon shines bright as I walk by
My family are singing in the echo of the night
Stars, I say, what a beautiful sight.

Everyone is happy
As we race past Mars
Big, bold planets
And dazzling stars.

Saturn looks elegant with its diamond-like rings
Shining and shimmering in the moonlight
Gliding past through space
The place where everything is night.

Zoë Grayer (10)
Garden House School, London

A Hocus Pocus Dream

Laughing and saying, 'Trick or treat!' all night,
A house surprised me all night.
I climbed up the stairs and rang the bell,
But a thunder of leaves came out of nowhere.
The Hocus Pocus sisters giggled around,
And evil-faced pumpkins spun around.
I felt excited but my friend scared,
It can't be them, they are dead!
The thunder stopped and I became one of them,
This was a Hocus Pocus dream.

Emma Lupi (10)
Garden House School, London

Cloud Dream!

I live above, I live below.
This is what you need to know.
Look at all the plants that grow.
Do you know where Mr Puff Puff goes?
No, I bet you don't.
Or are you begging to read his note?
OK, I'll tell you, you're the only one I'll tell.
Mr Puff Puff died in a well.
Well, not really, I did not kill him.
I did not use a sword.
I really actually sneezed him off the board!

Ilaria De Neiva Konig (10)
Garden House School, London

The Bushy Moustached Man

Beware!
Why?
Because the bushy moustached man
Is on the loose!
Aah, this is extremely terrifying,
How can I keep a happy face?
Not when the bushy moustached man
Is on the loose!

In my bed,
I dream of the bushy moustached man
Oh no! I am awake!
Big Ben strikes midnight
I am still awake
Oh no! I see a jet-black moustache
Gosh, it's the bushy moustached man!

Eva Lynch (8)
Garden House School, London

Once Upon A Dream

Once upon a dream,
All the children held hands and
treated each other equally.

Once upon a dream,
The people sang together and drank from
the same source.

Once upon a dream,
Discrimination did not ease and human rights flew
through the air.

Once upon a dream,
The children sang and stood in unison.

Once upon a dream,
I was there.

Christina Galani (10)
Garden House School, London

My Dream

I glide from cloud to cloud in the midnight sky
High above, houses so high
I dream about my unicorn night and day
Me and him just to play
The cloud will tickle us as we bang by
My unicorn is as wise as an owl
Catching the stars day and night
Up, up we go to space, not mace
No sign of light, no sign at all
Hearing silence is wonderful
All my worries disappear when I'm with him.

Sophie Cecil (10)
Garden House School, London

Magical Clouds

Step in my world and you will see magical, cute
unicorns with glittery horns.
There you will hear waterfalls relaxing, dripping down
to the hard ground.
Turn around and you will see a gigantic, glorious, fluffy
castle made of clouds.
You could sometimes see rainbows and slide on them.
This is an actual dream so if you go on an aeroplane,
Look at the clouds and you will see the castle
made of clouds.

Giulia Westermann (7)
Garden House School, London

The Beast

There was a beast,
Eyes like fire,
Claws like knives
And a tail like wire.

But his fur was fluffy,
His nose was wet,
His ears were floppy,
He could be my pet!

I happened to have,
A yummy treat,
He galloped over,
And took a seat.

I said, 'Hello!'
And shook his paw,
Now we'd be friends,
For evermore.

Max Viventi (10)
Garden House School, London

Fashion

Shiny, sparkly dresses and clothes so so pretty.
My goodness, I love fashion!
It's like a passion.
Everything I think of is clothes.
Do you like fashion?
Fashion is the best, it's never a test.
If you believe, you can achieve.
You can design clothes that are icy white!
Or you can design clothes that are fiery red!
My poem is a dream for my future fashion.

Flavia Galli-Zugaro (8)
Garden House School, London

Unicorns

U nique creatures with a mane as soft as candyfloss,
N eighing in the distance,
I n the night they come out and tiptoe through houses,
C areful not to make a peep,
O r the humans will know they're not imaginary,
R oaming through houses as quiet as mice,
N eighing when they get home,
S pectacular creature they really are.

Adriana Moretti (9)
Garden House School, London

Fiona

Wine, wine, Fiona gets drunk.
Jazz, jazz, Fiona helps, she even knows one jazz place.
Her wings are crystal clear like winter melting
into spring.
A beautiful emerald colour are her wings.
Crunchy peanut butter well helps.
Her pet dragon has rainbow scales like a
unicorn's horn.
Her dragon's beak has golden sparkles, so do not mess
with Fiona.

Julia Butter (9)
Garden House School, London

Untitled

I can see a village with people rushing around.
The houses all different
And the meringue with a hint of yellow
The men ran and the children, they watched
I saw a blue clue of a dog in the fog
Marshmallows off a body to the dolly
The arches all stared, full of fun made of lemon
meringues
A small bit of candy on the floor
I felt hungry
I looked and I was gone.

Alonga Case (9)
Garden House School, London

A Map Of Confusion

We live in a world of confusion.
We sleep in the day and work in the night.
Every day is just an opposite sight.
The clock strikes twelve when it's actually six.
Is life a blur or is it playing tricks?
Summer days are freezing cold,
and the winter moon is blazing gold.
It's a map of confusion, I've lost my way,
forwards or backwards, who's to say?

Jose Carlos Alvarez (9)
Garden House School, London

Once Upon A Dream

D reaming is like blowing in the sky,
R elationship is lovely like I'm running by,
E xciting like going to a fair,
A nd seeing a big, brown bear,
M ad like playing a game,
L ovely playing with a friend,
A wesome like jumping on a trampoline,
N ation a big blue sea
D ramatic acting like someone hit you.

Adnan Al-Sadi (8)
Garden House School, London

Once Upon A Dream

D reaming excellent things.
R idiculous jokes that people laugh at.
E xtraordinary trees with a chocolate trunk.
A mazing games that me and all my friends share.
M agical spells.
L ovely birds singing tunes.
A wesome tricks with skateboards.
N ice and kind people.
D elicious candyfloss as fast as a cloud.

Henry Butter (7)
Garden House School, London

Sweet World

In Sweet World the sweets shine brightly to the
glistening sun.
Sparkling candy canes swirl on cars.
When thunder strikes, it is like electric popcorn.
I am with my smart brother.
Dazzling chocolate falls.
Cuddly marshmallows fall.
Fizzy cold cola pools spray and go *kapang*.
The sloshing river goes *bang*.
The yummy sweets change.

Thomas Bradkin (7)
Garden House School, London

Above

M aybe there's a land far up high in a cloud,
A magical creature guardian guarding now,
G oo dee dum, the password is goo dee dum,
I n the clouds, elves chant and chant a poem,
C rystal Eye Crystal Angel come and see me tonight,
A little boggy music comes on and the fires starts,
L et light live.

Joy De Selancy (8)
Garden House School, London

The Haunted House

The door is made out of a large spider.
The doorknob is an eyeball as sticky as goo.
When you close the door, it goes *slam!*
At night you hear *stump, stump!*
Big foot!
 A witch made a poison, *pop, bang, fizz!*
Now lay your sleepy heads and go to bed.
You don't know what monsters will eat you then!

Starla Delucy Mckeeve (7)
Garden House School, London

Up, Up And Away

I glimpsed the colours blue and green
I had no idea when I was going to get out
of this dream
In the sky, a shooting star
I could not see it that well, I don't know why
I am embarrassed to say Uranus is lying on its side
But I say that with pride
I saw the sun out the corner of my eye
It's blinding bright, my oh my.

Valentine Matussiere (10)
Garden House School, London

Heaven!

Minions, rainbows, marshmallow clouds,
Unicorn and chocolate waterfall,
that is what I call Heaven
It is the perfect weather for picnics and riding unicorns
With our friends drinking from the chocolate waterfall
Watching Pegasus fly across the rainbow
Especially sliding down the slippery rainbow
Now this is what I call a cool land.

Carlotta Sofer (10)
Garden House School, London

Unicorn In The Sky

Once upon a time,
In a faraway rhyme,
I saw a unicorn,
Flying through the sky.

Its rainbow-coloured wings,
Danced in the blue yonder
In and around the whipped-up clouds,
Which were full of wonder.

I gracefully joined it,
Having extreme fun,
I was in high spirits,
As we passed by the sun.

Sofia Vialli (9)
Garden House School, London

Candles

Candles flickering with delight, bright amongst the
evening light.
Its golden reflection, triumphant of introspection.
Glowing, shining, bursting into flame, perseverance is
what we aim.
Dancing to the wind, its eerie shadow.
Everyone has their own candle and each is
one of a kind.
Come along now, for we have some friendships to bind.

Olympia Thieme Del Rio (10)
Garden House School, London

My Home

I am a warm and cosy dog,
I live in a house of glistening chocolate shortbread,
I have a marshmallow gate which
makes me feel hungry,
Sometimes I am so hungry that I
eat the delicious house,
My friends have a palace,
But I like my house,
Soon, I got a lovely chocolate fountain,
Which I liked much more than what I had.

Orlando White (8)
Garden House School, London

Kitten

Down in New York City,
In the centre of Central Park,
I found an abandoned kitty,
Alone in the dark.
It was such a pity,
It filled me with sadness,
So I took it home,
And it filled me with gladness.
I called him Harrow,
As my heart melted with happiness,
I glared down the narrow
Winding streets of Brooklyn.

Emma Grant-Diaz (11)
Garden House School, London

Playing

As the other puppies played, I asked a question
If I could play but they didn't let me
So I barked and growled and they got scared
For a tiny dog like me to be that scary
So they let me play and I howled with joy
So we ran and ran and ran until I was out of breath
And fell to the ground and fell asleep, and
others did too!

Sebastian Waring (7)
Garden House School, London

Winning Gold

In 2024, my family saw me win gold for
my very own team
Which made me feel I was living a dream.
My face shone as much as the sun,
Well, it was me who actually won.
When I landed on the floor,
I was unsure whether I was the one.
Well, I now know,
If you believe, you can achieve and
gymnastics is fantastic.

Lola Kandrac (9)
Garden House School, London

The Adventure

In Candyland the clouds are as soft as candyfloss.
When thunder strikes, it rains sweet candy.
The pool is made out of Fanta and all it thinks about
is Santa.
Umbrellas are candy canes red and white.
The people say that pigs are as pink as lipstick.
The trees are tall as talking balls.
The dogs fly up in the sky.

Mickey Maurus (7)
Garden House School, London

Cotton Candy Land

Cotton Candy is the best
Of course, it is better than the rest
To our king and queen we thank them
The best candy is cotton candy
Over the day we make candyfloss
Never we stop
'Cause it is amazing
And it's pink pop
No, we only eat cotton candy
Dinnertime is candyfloss
Year over, goodbye!

Paula Muth (8)
Garden House School, London

Dashing With Fairies

I'm dashing and I'm swaying with the clear, light, fluffy, blue sky.
I can feel the wind pushing me to another cloud with the fairy.
I'm just on the wing of a fairy.
Then popped a bottle of sparkling, fizzy water.
And let me tell you, it did not go well.
I banged my head and went to bed.

Olivia Simich (8)
Garden House School, London

Dream Coming True

Once upon a dream,
The sun creating a beam,
On the luscious green,
Oh, wondrous, wondrous unicorns,
A strip of gold wherever they run,
Making their tails scarily long,
Catch one, take one, bring one home,
Making the dark forest glow,
Make one a pet,
Take care of it,
Wherever they go.

B B Yanicelli (10)
Garden House School, London

Actress

Action, cameras, all the set!
Paparazzi, fame and autographs.
True love, romance, even though some actors maybe
have never even met,
Producers, cast, dark halls to film in.
Cameras smile and wink and giggle,
Microphones all around.
So your fans can hear you better,
In the best film around!

Helena Titherington (10)
Garden House School, London

Untitled

In my dream I smelt freshly-cut grass floating into
my nose.
I could hear nothing but the drop of an apple falling off
a tree nearby.
I could see the happy children playing around me.
I could taste fresh air just raising in me.
I could feel the smooth but bumpy tree behind me.

Maia Hewson (10)
Garden House School, London

Unicorn And I!

Unicorns in the forest,
Running on the forest ground,
I found,
A friend, a mythical friend,
Passing through the day,
We are on our way,
A river, a river,
What to do,
Get on my back,
With your sack,
Unicorns in the forest,
Running on the forest ground.

Savanna Snell-Dyson (8)
Garden House School, London

I Wonder When It Is Halloween

A magical day is nearly here,
It's Halloween, when creatures appear!
It's very scary with monsters all around.
It's a good day to scream and shout!
Scary dragons in the house,
Scary things all around.
Sadly, it was just a dream,
I wonder when it is Halloween.

Farah Parviz (8)
Garden House School, London

The Magical Ballet Shoes

B eautiful
A ll glittery
L iving
L ively
E nclosed
T ightly

S hoe
H umble
O pen
E mbracing
S urrounding

This poem is about a house made out of a ballet shoe.

Sophia ElBishlawi (10)
Garden House School, London

A Moon

I dreamt of a moon,
A moon far, far away.
People could not walk there,
But would have to sway.
A moon where your dreams would come true,
The ones about Star Wars and the ones about Ms Doo.
After a night it would bring you home,
To play with your toy set of mini Rome.

Igor Sagiryan (10)
Garden House School, London

The Windy Castle

The house was made from mysterious winds.
The doors were made from disappearing
glorious rainbows.
The roof was made from winking tornadoes.
The statues winked and blinked until
their work was done.
The beds danced like dancing elephants.
Pow, fizz, pop!

Purdy Lenigas (7)
Garden House School, London

Space

The open and vast space amazes me every time.
I raise my eyes and face to the ever so arcane enigma.
The waiting stars are as big as a sigma.
But they won't be waiting for long when I ascend from
the Earth.
Though stars are not tangible, I can still make contact.

Ramzi Kallini (11)
Garden House School, London

Daddy, Fluffy And Me!

Step inside my dreamland and you will see a candy
house with only two rooms.
Me, Daddy and Fluffy could not find some food so we
ate some of the house.
Me, Daddy and Fluffy saw Pegasus,
we stroked Pegasus.
Me, Daddy and Fluffy went back to the candy house
and went to bed.

Taylor Demong (7)
Garden House School, London

Dreamland

In Dreamland, there are people called the Imes.
Everyone lives in The Marshmallow Castle with
doors of solid chocolate.
The chocolate sun smiles over the land.
In Dreamland the people are made of Fanta.
When a storm strikes, it's OK because it rains candy.

Kiyaan Nathoo (8)
Garden House School, London

My Dad's Exploding Underpants

In the morning, I hear a *bing, bang, boom!*
Every morning I hear a *clang, clash, crash!*
On Sundays I hear *eeee, aaaah, awwww!*
Sometimes I think it's a cow but it's just my dad
Very sad
So I say, 'Cheer up, Dad!'

Alexander Sagiryan (8)
Garden House School, London

What Are Dreams?

Oh dreams, how do they come?
I dream about dragons, ships and bottles of rum.
Where do they come from? Where do they go?
Have they been dreamed of a long time ago?
Am I in a dream so brutally clear?
Is life a lie, like all the things I hold dear?

Caspian Primrose (11)
Garden House School, London

My Olympic Dream

My Olympic dream is bold and wild
I am the next Simone Biles
She's made to win and not to lose
She got girl power in gymnastics moves
I'll be just like her
I'll rock the gym
I'll show you when I'm older and I will win.

Celia Child-Villiers (9)
Garden House School, London

My Wonderful Dream

In the end I finally found my fame.
It was time for me to get upon the stage, I felt nervous and scared.
I finally won and I was happy and joyful.
I had to go on the podium and I was first and
I felt proud.
I was as good as an Olympic gymnast.

Gurbani Garcha (8)
Garden House School, London

Flying

As I fly I see the sky
Why do I do this? I don't know why
I see my father soaring above the misty, cool water
My home is in sight
But I fight for a ride
Alone around the dome
My mood is calm as I go for the food
I am in a zoo.

Hugh Walsh (10)
Garden House School, London

Untitled

Under my feet I feel hot and cosy marshmallow,
I live in a house with golden sweets all over the place,
My door is made of shining Haribo,
I am as warm as a snail in my house,
I always have tiny ants scribbling in my house!

Sacha Abecassis (7)
Garden House School, London

My Imaginary World

I woke up and I was in a whole new world
And it was the most wonderful place
I had to be careful
So I didn't step in the hot chocolate path
The stones were sweeties
I picked one up and ate one.

Allegra Collins (7)
Garden House School, London

The Kitten With Some Mittens

There was a kitten
Who played with some mittens
She cuddled me
She was as warm as can be
And she loved to drink tea
She liked mice and to dance on ice.

Athina Vardinoyannis (8)
Garden House School, London

Ghost Attack

G raves that say RIP.

H aunting sounds.

O oooohhhhh!

S un is hidden.

T empting to run away screaming and I was freaked out!

Alban Nottin (7)
Garden House School, London

They...

They stand up high
Away in the sky
With the misty wind a'blow
Making life as white as snow.

Brilliant colours flash again
But blankness returns here, and then
They shiver, they stammer
An unknown language with terrible grammar.

What they were
I do not know
They were a blur
But seemed to grow.

What were they doing?
Where will they go?
But like a cow mooing
I woke up feeling low.

Of course this happens
With many dreams
Remember them when nappin'
Not while the sun beams.

Mika Hood (9)
Hill House International Junior School, London

Purple Togas

Once upon a time, once upon a dream,
There was an amazing thing, it was a time machine,
Invented by a girl whose name was Laura,
Laura had seen many things before,
Like a talking lamp and many mermaids and more.
But this was the first, it was quite exciting and fun,
And scary and surprising,
So, as soon as she could, she jumped in and saw,
That this time machine was new,
it hadn't been here before,
It started to move, it went faster and faster
until she felt sick,
She needed a plaster,
She opened the door,
And in purple jeans she knew it was key,
To not wear purple unless you're the emperor, you see,
It was too late, the emperor was there,
Laura had time to change but what would she wear?
There were some pins, there were some aprons,
So she made a dress quick,
The emperor walked by, Laura felt quite sick,
She jumped back in the machine,
And travelled through space,
When she got back, she thought about

her history essay,
She got an A* because it was on the Romans,
So here is some advice for that time,
Do not wear purple togas!

Maya Smith (9)
Hill House International Junior School, London

Once Upon A Dream

Once upon a dream, I saw Calm within herself
Drifting in her orchard, she came up to me
She was as still as the silence that was not to be
The birds sang, the world moved
But in a bubble containing tranquillity.

Once upon a dream, War came raging in
His anger had reached boiling, he was not to recover
He charged, oblivious to what damage he would create
But that was his speciality that I could not stop
He was powerful, I was not.

Once upon a dream, Happiness did conquer
The brazen, bright light, neon colours, smiles, clowns
But the depression was undercover,
lurking in the shade
No one did know of his future raid.

Once upon a dream, Sadness moaned in his
anaemic palace
Pain was present, Joy locked up
Whimpering souls helplessly lost
Caused sadistic laughter, which soon died out
Yet not soon enough

The shadows crowded over, I was awake again
But which dream was I living in?
I'd settle for Peace instead of Joy
But was there only one choice?
I did not know...

Arabella Scanlon (10)

Hill House International Junior School, London

Olympic Journey

The hustle and bustle of the Brazilian streets,
The cars zooming past me at lightning speed,
The exotic colours surrounding me,
The whole city is lit up brightly,
Everyone around me is smiling.

I arrived at the Olympic Games,
With nothing but a smile on my face,
The crowd was roaring and cheering me on,
But the gold was all I desired all along.

The gun had shot,
The race was on,
It was hard, the distance was long,
I was about to give up,
I was about to stop,
But I told myself to run, run, run.

It is when you have supporters,
It is amazing what you can accomplish,
I even thought I had an advantage,

One more step to go,
Soon I will own that gold,
There is no stopping me,
I will win this for sure.

Yes, I won the race,
You definitely should have seen my face,
Standing on the podium was me and my friends,
Hearing the National Anthem brought me joy,
And this is my end to my Olympic journey.

Ayla Siddiq (9)
Hill House International Junior School, London

My Cousins

In a week they will come, so they say,
Year after month after day,
I sound like I'm dumb,
That's not true, do those people have any clue?
Finally, my cousins came,
I took a picture and put it in a frame,
It will be so much fun,
We had fun in rain and sun,
Playing day and night, that sounds just right,
I love my cousins more than ever,
Aren't we clever,
We are together, that's love,
You see a lovely, blue dove,
If my cousins see this they will know I care,
I hope they will give me a loving stare.

Annalise Worraker (9)
Hill House International Junior School, London

My Faraway Kingdom

My faraway kingdom,
Great and tall.
Vast and fair,
Most of all.

There's no king,
Only me!
The ruler
Of all eternity.

Humongous feasts,
Nice and filling.
Our kingdom's nice,
So there's no killing.

I ride through the town,
On my charming, white horse.
Our restaurants delight,
With every course!

Education? No problem,
We've got it all here.
So take a seat
And I'll lure you in, dear!

Cate Conklin (9)
Hill House International Junior School, London

The Glittering Ocean

I look over the beach,
The waves calmly walk in, onto the soft, yellow sand,
Seaweed swift on the ocean's bottom,
Crabs clap their claws,
Dolphins squeak out loud,
Fish swim glamorously,
Kids squeal and run up and down the beach,
My feet feel the hot, sandy sand,
Whoosh! go the waves,
Cacoor! go the seagulls in the blue, sunny sky,
All I see is an amazing summer's day!
Then a final *cacoor* in my ear,
Awakes me from my slumber.

Chloe Stranger (9)
Hill House International Junior School, London

The Beach Shell

I was at the beach all the same
As usual with my friends playing a game
Then we found a shell
And its colour was caramel
And we all had a scream but we were all a team
The shell was as bright as the sun's light
It was so magic that we'll never forget
And then we were so proud that we sang aloud
We found a shell and it was all caramel
This was so much fun
That it was so annoying when it was done.

Ines Baud (9)
Hill House International Junior School, London

A Dream In Blue!

As I sleep,
Creatures sleep,
As I dream,
These things I see,
Bluebells,
Bluebirds,
Everything in blue,
Am I like you?
Blue monsters,
Blue balls,
Everything possible in blue!
Blue,
Blue,
Blue,
All I dream about...
Blue!

Meira Gerasimovaite (9)
Hill House International Junior School, London

Once Upon A Dream

Once upon a dream,
All seemed to gleam,
When I entered a world,
Happiness went along the land, twirled!

Once upon a dream,
Fairies went around, all in a team,
There the rainbow with its pot of gold,
All the kings, old but bold!

Once upon a dream,
People in rain but still keen,
The rain, oh the rain,
Like crystals dropped by God!

Once upon a dream,
I looked up into eternity,
And it looked at me,
It said, 'Oh, you have seen our world,
Now you must awake!'

Vaatsalya Swarup (9)
Lucas Vale Primary School, London

Once Upon A Dream

When I dream
It could be about a stream
Or even a lake
In a windmill where you can bake.

I dream I am a superhero
And no one can overcome me
So when I have defeated the baddy
I end the day full of glee.

I dream I'm the absolute best
Better than every superhero
Because when I claim my victory
My powers seem to grow.

When I am ill, my pets help save the day
With their powers they heal me with their super ray
In Dreamland I heard the sound of a horn
And before my eyes is a magnificent unicorn.

I can dream I am rich
And have more than a wealthy witch
I am a powerful wizard
More amazing than a camouflaging lizard.

In my dream I can control a dragon
Whilst riding one-handed on a golden waggon
The flaming beast in comparison to me is weak
He is so mad he is a killer freak!

I dream I can rap, dance and sing
When on stage my performance is amazing
When I am racing I have to win ASAP
I will outrun everyone, leaving them behind
a whole lap.

Then I go back to sleep
I dream that I can leap
Over one million sheep.

Amiri Simpson (9)
Lucas Vale Primary School, London

My Wonderland

My family is trapped in the rubble
My voice calls out but to no avail, no reply reaches
my ears
My hands are searching, forever searching
But I feel nothing but the roughness of broken bricks
No soft skin, no smooth hair, just rough bricks.

Thoughts are running through my mind
Thoughts of sorrow, of times gone by and of all
thoughts despair
Where's my family, will I see them again?
Will I hear their voices calling my name?
And will I hear laughter again?
Will I feel the warmth of their skin against mine as I
hug them?
The softness of their face as I kiss them goodnight
Or will I ever get to see my cousin cry every time he
falls over?

I need to find my family so I can hold them, comfort
them, make them laugh
I need to be here so they will know how much
they're loved
How much they were missed while I was gone
I need her to look after me as I get older and to
brighten my day

And when they visit me after they've moved out from my house to build a new house for themselves and their future family to come.

Jordan Charles (10)
Lucas Vale Primary School, London

My Dream Adventure

One dark night when I was all alone,
I was sleeping in my bedroom when I thought I heard
my phone,
I opened the window to get fresh air,
Then I saw my toy dragon fly off my chair.

It got bigger and bigger as it flew towards me,
It said, 'Do you want to go on an adventure, Jahmari?'
Then my eyes opened wide,
I said, 'Yes, I do not mind.'

I jumped on its back like a big rucksack,
We flew through the window,
And into the falling snow.

We flew in slow motion,
Over the Atlantic Ocean,
Over the pyramids of Giza,
I didn't even need a visa.

We flew over France,
With a very, very long glance,
At the Eiffel Tower,
And the wonderful flowers.

I enjoyed looking over the Taj Mahal,
And China, OMG, the Great Wall,
Then, before I knew it, I was back in my bed,
Waking up with a sleepy head.

I heard my mum call me,
'Breakfast is ready!'
I looked over at my dragon toy,
It winked at me and smiled with joy.

Jahmari McCalla (10)
Lucas Vale Primary School, London

Once Upon A Life

Once upon a dream,
There stood a tree,
That bounced and shook and slashed and took,
Oh, once upon a dream.

Once upon a star,
As fast as a car,
Beyond the galaxy far,
Oh, once upon a star.

Once upon a planet,
There lived a girl called Janet,
Who discoed and pranced as the night sky danced,
Oh, once upon a planet.

Once upon a tiger,
Who, of course, is more finer,
Than a wisp and a bat and some crisps, what a dish,
Oh, once upon a tiger.

Once upon a friend,
That will be there till the very end,
That will be there forever,
We will always be together.

Once upon a race,
We will stand face-to-face,
Don't open up the gate,
For that will be the end of the human race!

Mary Maina (10)
Lucas Vale Primary School, London

My World And Me

My head is the sun,
My hair is the sun's rays,
My eyes are the clouds,
My fingers are the raindrops,
My toes are the grass,
My legs are the buildings,
Mix it all together and I am...
My world.

My world is kind,
My world is helpful,
My world is tolerant,
My world is respectful,
My world is passionate,
My world is not mean,
My world is more than sweet,
And that world is
Me!

Aaralyn Abangma (8)
Lucas Vale Primary School, London

Carrot Cake Land

In Carrot Cake Land,
Where everyone feels grand,
My mummy, daddy and I,
Looked at the sky,
And noticed the sun,
Was as big as a pie,
We sat by the lake and had tea and cake,
Beyond the big mountain,
Where there was a small fountain,
It looked so fantastic it made me want to do
gymnastics!
But everyone understands,
The best in the world,
Is Carrot Cake Land!

Jasmine Musundi-Locke (9)
Lucas Vale Primary School, London

The Forest

'Why do you prance along to a tune?'
I asked the enchanted wood.
'I prance because there's magic in the air,
Sparkling as glitter should.'

'Why so happy,' I asked the forest,
'So happy in the breeze?'
'Because,' the forest smiled at me,
'My pink dress covers my knees!'

'Why do you dance to the rhythm of a song,
So majestic I watch for hours?'
And the forest clapped and said with glee,
'I dance for the beauty of the flowers.'

'Why do you sing,' I asked the forest,
'So peacefully in the breeze?'
And the trees grinned at me, 'It's nearly summer,
And I will get back my leaves.'

'Why do you laugh?' I asked the forest,
'Can you share the joke?'
'Well!' giggled the forest, 'I scared the sun,
As my branches gave him a poke.'

'Why does the phoenix like you so much,
And the birds have a small chat with you?'
'I am so peaceful they cannot resist,
And, besides, they like my food!'

'Why do you whisper forest?
Is it because your sweet bird will wake?'
'No, it is because
The deadly wild animals need a break!'

'Do your leaves fly as the beautiful seasons go by?
Is that why you're so bored?'
'My leaf friends fly away each year,
Because I did something bad, forgive me Lord.'

'Don't you die of the snow?' I asked the forest,
'Or ever catch a cold?'
'I run through the air to warm myself up,
And the clouds my branches hold.'

'Why do you whisper through cold days gone past?'
I asked the forest one day.
'To send messages to my fellow friend,
And his name is tree Ray.'

'Why do you hate everyone?' I asked the forest,
'Is it because of your frown?'
'No, it's because they're dumb,
And they try to cut me down!'

Napoleon Class (10)
Merton Abbey Primary School, London

Mystical Unicorns

'Why do you give magical sparkles?' I asked
the unicorn,
'Because I don't believe in bad spirits!
I dance on rainbows because I need to send
wonderful dreams!'

'How do you send wonderful dreams?' I asked
the unicorn,
'And why do you do that?'
'Dance and I make a portal which shows all the kids,
I do that because they can learn more!'

'Why do you sing?' I asked the unicorn,
'Such a sweet and happy tune?'
'Because,' the unicorn smiled!

'Why do you laugh?' I asked the unicorn,
'And how can you laugh?'
'I laugh because it makes other people laugh!
I just move my mouth,
And it's good to always be happy!' the unicorn laughed.

'Why do you dance !' I asked the unicorn,
'I dance because it makes me smile!'

Alexandra Vicovan Ioana (10)
Merton Abbey Primary School, London

Untitled

Once upon a dream,
Not far away,
Down by the streets,
Where the little girl lay,
All was calm,
All was fine,
All was well,
All was nice,
Silence in the street,
No one's awake,
Everybody's asleep,
It's no mistake,
There's an imaginative world,
Not far from here,
Close your eyes and
Things will magically appear,
Hold on tight, take my hand,
I'm taking you off to a faraway land,
It's a place you'll love,
It's full of fun,
So don't keep it waiting,
Come on everyone!
Welcome everyone, our journey's complete!
Walking, talking, giant snuggly teddy bears

you will meet.
Look at the chocolate fountains,
Look at the marshmallows,
The people, the houses,
Oh, what a sight to see!
Down the lane is a gingerbread shop,
So you can buy them whenever you please.
Receive £50,000 a week at the bank,
Meet Goostarph and his pals who are
always pulling pranks!

Evana Otabil (9)
Merton Abbey Primary School, London

My Dream Is Crazy!

Your Nyan cats are stealing my puppy cotton candy!
Well, they do have crazy minds!
Your slushy tree is very refreshing!
Thanks my friends, and my amazing teacher helped me make it!

Your rainbow money roller coaster is holding puppies and kittens!
That's only because Grumpy Cat controls
the roller coaster!
Can you help me find the unicorn express bus?
Sure! I will always help you!

Where is McDonald's with all yummy foods and drinks?
It's right over there, it is called Yum Yum Land!
Can I visit your dancing chocolate friends?
Sure! Go through the portal and you will boom and zoom straight to them!

I have one more wish before this fantastic and fun dream ends.
What's that, my friend?
I want to remember you next time I sleep and dream!
Just say the magic word please and this wish will become true!

Raulis Barsegianas (10)
Merton Abbey Primary School, London

Dreamtopia

Once upon a dream, I saw a bus that went to space
I did not know why or where it went
One day, I caught it so I could see what happened
behind the scene.

So I hopped, skipped and jumped on it
Then I saw the amazing world of Avalor!
So I saw rainbows beyond my wildest dreams
I said to myself, 'I'm staying here!'

I cannot detest, this world is brilliant!
The sky is smiling down at me
The world is perfect and kind of mad
With marshmallow cannons and wondrous rainbows!

I have a wondrous candy house over there
But there's one thing missing
My mum, my cat and my rat
My mum smiles like the sun
My cat is like a tiger and my rat is very fat.

So I went on the wondrous train of mystery
I went home to my mum, my cat and my rat
To make history!

India Francis (9)
Merton Abbey Primary School, London

Untitled

Once upon a dream,
A deserted land was green,
In the howling, windy breeze,
A magical portal has been seen.

The portal ruthlessly sucked us inside,
And took us to Imagination Land,
We went spinning and swirling like a tornado,
In the vivid, vibrant rainbow.

As soon as we arrived,
A crazy man had cried:
'Hey everyone, new citizens!'
'What?' said the people, 'More villagers?'

'We're not villagers,' we said in frustration,
'We are citizens!' we said, correcting.

Where there was joy there were people,
We wished for it and it came to life!
'Remember, you can visit this land anytime,
You just have to use imagination!'
We said as we lived happily ever after in this
mystical, magical land.

Dele Oyeyele (10)
Merton Abbey Primary School, London

I Live In A Pudding

Once upon a dream
I saw a colourful adult unicorn
And then, a few days later, I found some
rare rainbow unicorns.

The thunder clouds rain chocolate
There's a three-headed lion that flies
The cannons are made out of chocolate.

There's fireflies that light up like a rainbow
There are cotton candy unicorn decorations
That you can eat on your caramel roller coaster.

My house is a giant marshmallow
There are magical walking
gingerbread men everywhere
There's only gummy bear furniture!

There's whipped cream on top
And there's a cherry on top
There's also a toffee door that
grows back when you eat it
And then you can eat it again and again.

Jayden Brewster (9)
Merton Abbey Primary School, London

Pure Imagination Dream

Why are you in my head?
When I'm in my bed
Even though you're fake
You still make me ache.

What do you mean?
Why are you mean?
If you don't want a dream
Don't be green.

Who are you making me?
A crazy dreaming me
A little boy who loves dreams
Can make a huge, roaring feat.

The dream I created
Will be much better than you
So listen up and try not to sleep
In my modern mansion.

Has five amazing animals
That slurps up chocolate milk!
That makes their tongue fizzy
With a secret path into a football pitch.

Where people scream my name
And sing Man United's anthem
And I score ten goals every time
And they scream, 'Goal!'

Levi Jordan Alfie Samuels (9)
Merton Abbey Primary School, London

Untitled

Moon spoon I included in my dream
Even though you fake it, you still make me laugh
In my dream, when I launch to Dreamland,
everything will change
Nothing will ever touch me.

After I went to my room in Dreamland
I found out you can't dream in Dreamland
Because you will be in another dream
Then the flaming, burning sun told me that
if you hurt someone
You will be kicked out of Dreamland
but he was kidding.

Suddenly, when you are on another dream,
it is all chocolate
Me and my friends ate all the chocolate
Then it came again and we ate until we were full
We went swimming and that's what happened.

Adam Victory (10)
Merton Abbey Primary School, London

The Mermaid Dream Under The Sea

Once upon a dream,
I imagined a world with mermaids dancing and
prancing in the ocean.
'What do you see in your dream?' I asked the mermaid.
'A lovely person and a magic tree,' she said.
'I dance and prance to any music I seek.'
'Why are you singing?' I asked the mermaid.
'Because someone first invited me to a party, you see.'
'Why are you darkening?' I asked the mermaid.
'It says on my shell phone the party has just finished.
I'm late, you see.'
'Don't worry, I'll make a party just for you and me!'
'Thanks, you're the best friend forever!'

Kize Williams (9)
Merton Abbey Primary School, London

Sweetlandia

In Sweetlandia
Where M&Ms rain every day
People use chocolate coins
The grass is as yummy as sugar

Where Haribo is medicine
The talking lifts go everywhere
Fanta-powered cars are made
Soda-powered motorbikes are also made

And melon city
Where people have hot heater of candy
Melon juice is made in two seasons
Pizza juice is always open

And dancing strawberries
Where ice cream gums exist
People drink from the soda fountain
Healthy corner is always there

This is Sweetlandia!

Tharun Yogendram (9)
Merton Abbey Primary School, London

Dreams

D reams, they're nightmares and fun, happy dreams based on your favourite things, so one night I had this dream. I was thinking about ants, chickens and animals. I was having so much fun, it felt like real life!

R ight, you don't always get fun things like you get nightmares so, even if you're having a good dream, it can turn bad. Who knew animals are so rude sometimes?

E xciting, sometimes for me it gets very exciting because it leaves me on a cliffhanger.

A ll dreams are different, scary and fun.

M any dreams are so enjoyable.

Mersedesa Barsegianaite (9)
Merton Abbey Primary School, London

You And Your Pet Marshmallow!

Imagine a mega modern mansion with a special room
to go to Candy Land!
Every day in your flower bed, there are 30 lollipops and
ice lollies in them.
Only in one day they grow.
They always smile at you if you come outside.

Once you see a unicorn in your special room,
You see a mark on the unicorn,
It was a moon, not any moon, it was a shiny and
beautiful moon.

You ask the unicorn what its name is,
She says, 'My name is Marshmallow!' in a happy voice.
And you say, 'Do you want to be my little fellow?'

Sara Salah (9)
Merton Abbey Primary School, London

Candy Man

Once upon a dream
I was very green
I saw a candy man
With some sandy tan
I asked, 'What do you do?'
'I grow candy in my land'
'Who are you?'
'I am a candy man.'

Boom! What is it?
It is a new species growing
Come on, let's see
Laughing candy has grown
Oh no
What is it?
We will hear laughing forever.

Oh no, I have to leave soon
Why?
Because it's nearly early morning
Eat some candy before you go
Oh no, I have to go.

Jaydhidh Yogeswaran (9)
Merton Abbey Primary School, London

Mystical Land

Once upon a dream, I walked into a mystical land,
I saw all the Pegasuses playing in the sand,
Chocolate fountains 'splash' they said,
There's the galaxy stars glittering above my head.

Whistling wind and rainbows above every day,
Ice cream houses and all-candy pools,
The unicorns as magnificent as the shining sun,
In this land everyone has won.

Playing with flying deer,
Never dropping any tears,
You can fly as high as the sky,
I know I'll be visiting this fantasy again!

Carmel Francis (9)
Merton Abbey Primary School, London

All About My Dreams

Once upon a dream, at night everything was dark,
And the moon was shining,
While the stars lit up the bumpy, old road.
When it was morning, the sun was shining as bright
as a headlight
And the beautiful flowers were blooming very slowly,
And when I felt the breeze of the wind,
I could feel nature.
I could feel the autumn leaves peacefully fall on me,
And the air felt so relaxing and the huge tree
was perfect
To get some shade when it's hot or cold.

Aliyan Ahmad (9)
Merton Abbey Primary School, London

Once Upon A Dream...

Once upon a dream...
There was a princess
Who was daughter of Jesus
They were living in a house
That was made up of candyfloss
Unicorns were roaming around
How good that day was.

Princess flew with the unicorns to the clouds
And she saw her cutest house
The other unicorns followed her
They were really like her
Princess took one of the tickling cotton candy clouds
It was really delicious too
But it was time to go home...

Hira Isik (10)
Merton Abbey Primary School, London

Sweetlandia

In Sweetlandia where sweets rain
There are ice cream video games
Yummy soda fountains
And the candyfloss hotels.

Where Haribo is medicine
And soda-powered motorbikes are made
And candy-powered roller coasters dance.

The cheese-filled moon and rockets flying
There are people waiting for candy too
Imagine a house full of candy
A soda fountain, a candy park and a Haribo hospital
With Haribos to give you energy.

Cadey Moore (9)
Merton Abbey Primary School, London

Maybe

Maybe I will be a footballer,
And score the winning goal.
Maybe I will be a fireman,
And slide down the fireman's pole.

Maybe I will be a scientist,
And do loads of crazy tests.
Maybe I will be a waiter,
And serve lots of different dishes.

Maybe I will be an athlete,
And run one hundred miles.
Whatever I choose to be when I grow up,
Will have to make me smile.

George Brown (9)
Merton Abbey Primary School, London

Dream On

D ancing pandas, singing pigs is what it holds.
R acing, vrooming cars let it unfold.
E xamine pugs with six feet long tongues full of puns.
A piece of Lego going bang, also a fluttering fan.
M aybe a friendly giant tucks you asleep.

O ver and over and over again, dream till your
N ew heart's content.

Peter Sam Newell (9)
Merton Abbey Primary School, London

My Dream

Boom! Zoom!
I launched into my dream as fast as a jet
Even faster than a bullet as big as a rocket
I launched into Dreamland where everything is just how
I like it.

In Dreamland, the sky is as blue as can be
Grey clouds have never appeared
No fight, no wars
We always smile just like our big, yellow, dancing sun.

Khalid Dore (10)
Merton Abbey Primary School, London

My Dream

M y dreams are sometimes...
E xciting,
N ever-ending,
A dventurous!

K een thoughts...
A re a pathway to a spectacular dream,
M agic is everywhere,
R emember,
A ny dream,
N ever dream the past,

Dream the
Future...

Mena Kamran (9)
Merton Abbey Primary School, London

Unicorn World

Once upon a dream,
When I woke up I saw a colourful rainbow,
Shining over my house,
Made of candy doors, gummy bear roof
And chocolate walls with muffin room.

As the sun danced and smiled on Earth,
Bang, crash, boom! went the chocolate bullets
Then exploded with candy everywhere!

Kiril Bozhilov (9)
Merton Abbey Primary School, London

Why Do You

Why do you shine in the summer?
Do you smile when you shine?
I smile all the time
I shine in the summer because it is the best time.

Why do you sparkle in winter?
Why do you spit all over us?
I like winter because it is nice and cold
I spit on you because kids like snow.

Malek Barnett (10)
Merton Abbey Primary School, London

Candy House

Once upon a dream
I saw a world full of candy
I went inside and stole some candy
What are you?
I am a candy house.

Then I jumped and caught a cloud
And gingerbread men fell out
I saw a walking gingerbread coming to me
They told me I could eat them.

Joanne Obeh (9)
Merton Abbey Primary School, London

I Want To Be A Teacher

Teachers reach the children, they're
teaching, shaping brains,
Creating goals and aims,
Answering questions without hesitation
Teaching is like planting seeds
That grow into trees
And, one day, I will be the tree
Planting all the seeds.

Heavenly Critcher (9)
Merton Abbey Primary School, London

Untitled

Once upon a dream,
I woke up and saw,
A beautiful rainbow,
And flying unicorns.

Then I saw a rainbow house,
With unicorns inside having a party,
Then I saw dancing clouds and a dancing sun,
And went inside to join the party.

Erdet Dedushi (9)
Merton Abbey Primary School, London

Bike

It has two wheels
Nice and strong
I pass the hills
It never goes wrong.

I ride my bike every day
To the school and back home
When I speed up, my mum says,
'Don't cross the road alone!'

Gabriel Hreniuc (8)
Merton Abbey Primary School, London

In My Dreams

I love unicorns
All different colours and bright
I dream of unicorns
When I am sleeping at night
She flies through the sky with a glittering glow
Sometimes she turns the colour of pearl-white snow.

Sadie Marsham (9)
Merton Abbey Primary School, London

Dreams

At night-time I thought about a baby hedgehog
And I thought that it was throwing spiky balls
And I was running away and I nearly stabbed him
But then I thought that all I can do is make a home.

Goncalo Monteiro (8)
Merton Abbey Primary School, London

Dreamy Days

I am running on the green grass
I am wearing a club shirt
I am hearing people screaming my name
I am looking at the best goalkeeper
And I am aiming to score a goal.

Patryk Slusarczyk (9)
Merton Abbey Primary School, London

Happy

The nice feeling,
The cool breeze on your face,
The heart of joy,
The smile that is from ear to ear,
The shine on your eyes is a sun.

Layla Al-Bayati (8)
Merton Abbey Primary School, London

Sunshine

Lovely - warm
Bright - yellow
Relaxing - hot
Beaming - smiling
Better than any
Other sunshine
I miss you.

Pola Czekaj (9)
Merton Abbey Primary School, London

Everywhere I Go!

Everywhere I go, I ride on my horse.
Everywhere I go, I win races.
Everywhere I go, I will love the world!!

Cherry Bernard (9)
Merton Abbey Primary School, London

Reading

Reading
Inspirational, likeable
Loads of pages
Makes you read it
Colourful.

Aran Amin (9)
Merton Abbey Primary School, London

Untitled

In my head
A dog jumped in the air
And back down
He went without
Any pain.

David Tyczynski (9)
Merton Abbey Primary School, London

Disneyland

Disneyland
Fun, epic
Super fun with
Family, cool entertainment
Amazing.

Kacey Fisher (9)
Merton Abbey Primary School, London

Mum

Kind
Caring, funny
Loveable, fun, mardy,
Amazing, good
Wonderful.

Charlie Fraser (9)

Merton Abbey Primary School, London

To The Mountaintop!

Walking with my husky dog,
In the morning, dancing fog,
From the garden frozen fountains,
I can see the biggest mountains.
And one day I have a hope,
To climb to the mountaintop,
I'm going to parachute down,
But I know I'm not going to get the crown.
Could I be in a stream,
Sinking down into a dream?
Maybe run out of breath,
Nervous and scared to death.
Landing in a big pile of snow,
Which is as soft as a pillow,
And I should have known,
It was all a dream.

Ana Maria Dumitru
St John's Walworth CE Primary School, London

Unicorn Poem

Unicorn, unicorn, beautiful unicorn.
You're so colourful like a rainbow.

Unicorn, unicorn, pretty unicorn.
You're so pretty like a piece of beautiful cheese.

Jamila Ricketts (7)
St John's Walworth CE Primary School, London

YoungWriters
Est.1991

YOUNG WRITERS INFORMATION

We hope you have enjoyed reading this book – and that you will continue to in the coming years.

If you're a young writer who enjoys reading and creative writing, or the parent of an enthusiastic poet or story writer, do visit our website **www.youngwriters.co.uk**. Here you will find free competitions, workshops and games, as well as recommended reads, a poetry glossary and our blog.

If you would like to order further copies of this book, or any of our other titles, then please give us a call or visit **www.youngwriters.co.uk**.

Young Writers
Remus House
Coltsfoot Drive
Peterborough
PE2 9BF
(01733) 890066
info@youngwriters.co.uk